faithfulness

A Highly Favoured Life Devotional

Table of Contents

Dedication

This devotional is dedicated to the countless number of faithful Christians that we have watched year after year standing strong for the Lord. Thank you for not wavering in your convictions and labor in ministry.

Introduction

Great is Thy faithfulness, O God my Father
There is no shadow of turning with Thee
Thou changest not, Thy compassions, they fail not
As Thou hast been, Thou forever will be

Pardon for sin and a peace that endureth
Thine own dear presence to cheer and to guide
Strength for today and bright hope for tomorrow
Blessings all mine with 10,000 beside

Great is Thy faithfulness
Great is Thy faithfulness
Morning by morning new mercies I see
All I have needed Thy hand hath provided
Great is Thy faithfulness
Great is Thy faithfulness
Great is Thy faithfulness, Lord, unto me

What a hymn! It is said that Thomas Chisholm wrote these words not out of a traumatic situation, but during everyday "normal" life. He knew God's faithfulness daily. It seems that he woke every morning seeing new mercies, as the song goes. What an amazing testimony of God's goodness.

We know beyond a shadow of a doubt of God's faithfulness to us, but what about our faithfulness to Him? Do we make promises to God that we have no intention of keeping? Do we step back from biblical standards we have been taught to fit in with the world's standards? Do we choose to ignore blatant sin while watching a movie or reading a magazine? Are we quick to like a post on social media that may not be pleasing to the Lord? The list can go on and on.

This devotional is meant to remind you of God's faithfulness and encourage you to stay faithful to Him! Keep in mind that you influence others with your testimony of faithfulness! We hope that this book encourages you to step away from the cares of the world and be challenged to thank God for His unending faithfulness to you and remember your decision to faithfully serve Him.

- Callie Shiflett | Marissa Patton

Faithful to the Vow

By Grace Shiflett

---

*And she vowed a vow, and said, O LORD of hosts, if thou wilt indeed look
on the affliction of thine handmaid, and remember me, and not forget
thine handmaid, but wilt give unto thine handmaid a man child,
then I will give him unto the LORD all the days of his life,
and there shall no razor come upon his head.*

I Samuel 1:11

Vow: a promise to God; a thing promised.

In these verses, we read a familiar story of Hannah praying under a heavy burden. The Bible describes her burden as "bitterness of soul" in verse 10. In this agonizing prayer, she makes a vow to the Lord. If God would give her a baby boy, she would give him unto the Lord all the days of his life. As we read on through the chapter, we see the Lord gave her the son she prayed for. Now, she was faced with the realization that before long, the time would come for her to honor her vow.

I wonder how many times she had to remind herself while she was holding her precious Samuel close that she would need to stay faithful to the Lord and keep the vow she had made to her God. If we put ourselves in her place, we can only speculate that more than once, she second-guessed this vow. She might have even talked to the Lord again, attempting to get out of this vow. Possibly, she was strong and never doubted. The Bible does not let us know either way. What we do know clearly is that she set a great example by staying faithful to what she had promised.

What an amazing prayer Hannah prayed in 1 Samuel 2! One can almost feel the wonderful joy she had for the goodness of God in her life. This was a direct result of her staying faithful to the vow she made. Imagine how she must have felt every year when she brought him the new little coat that she had made for him (I Samuel 2:19)! She must have thought, "No regrets! I am so glad I kept the vow I made."

What about us? Have we made vows to God, then showed a lack of faithfulness on our part to follow through? Maybe when it became difficult or was no longer convenient, we hesitated or simply refused to keep the promise we made?

Let us ask God to give us the strength we need to not just vow a vow. That is the easy part. We must be faithful to follow through so we can experience what Hannah experienced. She had her prayers answered. The joy of the Lord flowed in her life. She got to see God do supernatural things, all because she was faithful to keep the vow she made.

faithfulness

Passage

Today's
Date: _____

Prayers Requests

Notes

Faith in Action

By Belinda Young

But be ye doers of the word, and not hearers only, deceiving your own selves.

James 1:22

Jesus often spoke in parables using an understandable everyday truth and applied it to a much deeper and far more important truth.

Consider a very simple example of faithfulness. I make my bed every day whether I am at home or away or at someone else's house, whether I am healthy or whether I am sick. I cannot stand for my bed to be left unmade – the whole room is a mess – I cannot find anything – nothing I do flows – all I see is an unorganized mess.

It does not matter what other people think or what other people do. They may say that I am wasting my time, but my mind needs things organized. It takes two whole minutes to make my room look comfy and inviting by making up my bed. I can truly say that I am faithful in making my bed!

Let us apply that to far more important areas of life. Faith, what I believe with all my heart, cannot be seen. Faithfulness is the action that I do because of my faith – it can be clearly seen. Hebrews 11:1 says, "Now faith is the substance of things hoped for, the evidence of things not

13

FAITHFULNESS IS THE ACTION THAT I DO BECAUSE OF MY FAITH.

seen." You cannot see my faith, right? Oh, but you can! James 2:18 says, "Yea, a man may say, Thou hast faith, and I have works: shew me thy faith without thy works, and I will shew thee my faith by my works." You can totally see what I believe by what I do and how I behave. Faithfulness is my faith put into action. It does not matter whether anybody else thinks it is important or not. I do what I believe is important. Faith cannot be seen. It is a matter of the heart! Faithfulness is the action that reveals the faith in the heart!

James 1:22 says, "But be ye doers of the word and not hearers only, deceiving your own selves." If you are not doing what you say you believe, you really do not believe it. You will do what you really believe in your heart. You will choose what you believe – whether right or wrong. No one else can make that choice for you. Your actions will reveal what you have chosen to believe. Faithfulness is a choice you make on purpose. You may get slack, but because it is in your heart, you cannot stay slack, you will go back to doing what you believe in.

Proverbs 24:16 says, "For a just man falleth seven times, and riseth up again: but the wicked shall fall into mischief." I desire and strive to be faithful to the right things – things that would please God – things that promote me to be close to the Lord and encourage others to seek the Lord. Below are just a few examples of areas in our life that require faithfulness and each can be greatly expanded on:

- **My relationship with God**
  - Reading my Bible
  - Praying
  - Church attendance

- **My relationship with my family**
  - To love and honor my spouse
  - To love, teach, and nurture my children

- **My relationship with others**
  - My church family
  - Those in my community - they know who I am, but do not know me closely.
  - Complete strangers
  - Shining for the Lord Jesus to all those around in all I do

faithfulness

Today's
Date: _____

Passage

Prayers Requests

Notes

Influence of Faithfulness

By Andrea Leeder

Moreover it is required in stewards, that a man be found faithful.

I Corinthians 4:2

There is no One more faithful than our Lord Jesus Christ! What a great blessing it is to know Christ; and as a child of God, we can experience the faithfulness of God.

First of all, you can never experience the faithfulness of God if you have never trusted Christ as your Savior. If there has never been a time that you put your faith and trust in Christ, now is the time to accept Him as your Savior. Repent of your sin and trust Him. Only those that know Christ, can experience God's faithfulness.

Lamentation 3:22-23, says, "It is of the Lord's mercies that we are not consumed, because his compassions fail not. They are new every morning: great is thy faithfulness." No matter how many times we may fall short and become unfaithful in our walk with God and in so many other aspects of the Christian life, we can rest assured that God's promises are true.

We read of all the miracles in the Bible that God performed. It is amazing to think that the same God who performed those miracles, is the same God we serve today! He still performs miracles today. His faithfulness never ceases.

Are we as faithful to God as He is to us? The answer, if we were all honest, is no. Faithfulness on our part is a must to be a successful Christian. Others can tell whether or not we are walking with the Lord. We will walk in the flesh if we are not daily reading God's Word. It is easier to want to serve God if we are spending time with Him. We must take staying faithful to God seriously! We are all guilty of putting priorities before God. We let our busy lives get in the way of serving Him. Strive to please God and serve Him with your whole heart! No matter where we fall short, God makes a way for us to become better if we allow His Word to change us.

There have been many people who have influenced my life through faithfulness. I have watched people serving God in the ministry having so much fun. It was contagious and made me want to serve also! On the other hand, I have also seen those working in the ministry that made it seem like a chore. Do not be the kind of Christian that makes serving God look like a drudge.

Do not underestimate how much of an influence you can be to someone by staying faithful. My parents were missionaries. We, as a family, depended on the faithfulness of churches supporting us financially to be able to stay on the mission field. Your faithfulness matters! It does not matter what stage of life you are in. Your faithfulness, or lack of faithfulness, will influence someone.

Who are we influencing through our faithfulness to God?

Galatians 6:9, says, "And let us not be weary in well doing: for in due season we shall reap, if we faint not."

faithfulness

Today's
Date: _____

Passage
_____

Prayers Requests
_____

Notes
_____

Faith Like Noah

By Brittney Young

---

*By faith Noah, bring warned of God of things not seen as yet moved with fear,
prepared an ark to the saving of his house; by the which he condemned the
world, and became heir of the righteousness which is by faith.*

Hebrews 11:7

I love Bible stories. The older I get, the more I appreciate them and recognize how I can apply them to my life! Although there are so many stories in the Bible of people whose lives displayed such great faith, I would like to take a moment and focus on the faithfulness of Noah.

A few years ago, I had the opportunity to go to the Ark Encounter in Kentucky. It was amazing! I am a visual learner and having a real live replica of the ark to explore and walk around on was so fascinating! As I approached the ark and began walking up the ramp, tears automatically started coming to my eyes. The story of Noah became very real to me. As I walked through, I tried to imagine what he and his family must have gone through. I envisioned the long days and nights he labored! The callused hands, the aching body, the sunburned skin, the mockery, the loneliness, the discouragement, the lack of help, the lack of friendships, and the weariness his family must have endured for 120 years. Somehow, he set his eyes on the goal. None of these hardships, including fear, stopped him from doing what God said!

I have been saved now for almost twenty-two years and have been a pastor's wife for almost ten years. I do not know about you, but sometimes in my journey when life seems tough, I have used the phrase, "I feel like I am in a boat all by myself." When the dry times came, when it seemed all was in vain, when it seemed friendships were few, when weariness set in, I felt alone. But let's be honest, Noah and his family were literally in a boat all by themselves... well, except for a bunch of noisy, stinky animals, of course! I find comfort in Noah's situation and quickly come to my senses! I have not had to endure anything like Noah or any of the patriarchs of the faith have had to endure. But just as they were, I can be faithful in this journey that God has given to me.

One of my favorite parts of the Ark Encounter was seeing the realistic wax figures of Noah and his family gathered around an altar offering sacrifices to the Lord, which is the first thing they did when they got off the ark! Can you imagine the relief, the thankfulness they must have felt after coming through that storm together! All of those years of faithfulness paid off for Noah! Were they easy? No! But he found grace in God's eyes, and his family was saved! Which is exactly the desire of my heart!

I want faith like Noah!

NONE OF THESE HARDSHIPS STOPPED NOAH FROM DOING WHAT GOD SAID!

faithfulness

Today's
Date: _____

Passage _____

Prayers Requests _____

Notes _____

hf

Waiting Faithfully

By Sarah Russell

He hath made every thing beautiful in his time:

Ecclesiastes 3:11a

Psalm 104:27, says, "These wait all upon thee; that thou mayest give them their meat in due season."

Psalm 145:15, says, "The eyes of all wait upon thee; and thou givest them their meat in due season."

Where I live in the south, seasons are not always what you think they should be! Many a Thanksgiving, my family and I have sat around the back deck in short sleeve shirts, sipping on iced tea, and enjoying a slice of pumpkin pie. Definitely not the sweater weather you would expect. But that is the south we know and love!

Life is a lot like that. Seasons come, and seasons go. Oftentimes the season is unexpected. Sometimes, we are ready for a new season, and other times, we are begging the Lord to let this season last a little longer. Sometimes, it is a waiting season. Those seasons can be hard and frustrating.

I have been in a few different waiting seasons in my life. It can challenge your faithfulness to the Lord and His ways when He calls you to the waiting season. So, what are we supposed to do in these times? Well, the first thing to do is "be still." When God calls us to wait, we can be sure that it is for a divine purpose. Stay where you are and wait. Do not try and rush ahead of God's time.

Second is to continue being faithful to your daily relationship with Christ. Read and pray faithfully! Remind yourself that He has always been faithful to you and will continue to be.

Lastly, remain in the appointed work He has given you. Maybe that is teaching Sunday school, singing specials, caring for an elderly parent, or helping in ministries of your local church. Stay faithful in your work for Him.

Your waiting season may be waiting for a husband. Perhaps it is waiting for the Lord to bless you with a child. Maybe you are in a particularly hard season, and you are waiting for a new, more joyful time. Your waiting season will come to an end. And a new season will begin! If you have remained faithful in your time of waiting, just imagine how much more joyful your new season may be! In His time, in His way, and sometimes not in the way we expect, He brings joy. But His ways and His timing are always perfect. So, remain faithful, my sister! He is ever faithful, and He is always only good.

faithfulness

Today's
Date: _____

Passage

Prayers Requests

Notes

The Heart of the Matter

By Kate Ledbetter

Now faith is the substance of things hoped for, the evidence of things not seen.

Hebrews 11:1

Faithfulness, for as long as I can remember, has been defined by attendance. Church members showing up to church and staying has seemed to be the only requirement of which most take note. It is why people in horrible marriages (that they never work on) still get standing ovations for reaching yearly milestones. Or how someone who verbalized for years that they hated their job still retires with full benefits. To me, attendance does not describe this amazing word – faithfulness. Faithfulness has a depth that goes far beyond what you say or simply what you do on the outside. Faithfulness begins in the heart.

The Bible says, "Now faith is the substance of things hoped for, the evidence of things not seen" (Hebrews 11:1). Substance means "support or confidence." Things hoped for means "to expect or confide." Evidence means "proof or conviction." By these definitions, faith is the support for what we expect from God based on His Word. It is proof of what we cannot see.

31

For so long, it seems we keep trying to define the word faithfulness by what we can see. Maybe because it is all we can understand in our flesh. If our definition is always based on outward reflections, then we need to stop giving credence to lip service and start defining the faithful by what they do with God's Word. In this, we fully understand that we cannot see the heart. This is the evidence of things not seen. Faithfulness must be defined by obedience.

In Matthew 5, Jesus gives us a deeper look at simple obedience. Faithfulness is seen in our motives – why we do what we do, to begin with. Like the child who takes out the trash when told, all the while stomping and slamming doors, our obedience must be one of submission to The Lord and His Word, not actions with the wrong attitude. I challenge you to study Matthew 5 and look not at your outward actions but look deeper into your heart. Jesus shows that "thou shalt not kill" goes so much deeper than the murder (Matthew 5:21-26). He shows us how adultery can affect us in more ways than we bargain for (Matthew 5:27-32). This chapter gives us all a look at where faithfulness lies and challenges each of us to ask ourselves how obedient we really are to God. It continues into areas that can be a struggle for the strongest of Christians.

It is easy to say we love the Lord and others, but love is not found in unfaithfulness. Love is the gift we give, not the investment we make expecting a return. Faithfulness is the foundation of charity. Read Hebrews 11 and Matthew 5 and ask yourself, "how faithful am I really?" It is not about formulating something that man can see to make yourself look good. True faithfulness will show because of what lies inside. The evidence will speak for itself.

faithfulness

Today's
Date: _____

Passage

Prayers Requests

Notes

The Right Hand

By Dixie Sasser

For I the LORD thy God will hold thy right hand,
saying unto thee, Fear not; I will help thee.

Isaiah 41:13

It is estimated that 87% of the world's population is right-handed. Hebrew is written from right to left, as are many of the ancient languages. Some say that because most of the world's population was right-handed, the natural flow to chisel words in stone would be from right to left. Today, we place our right hand on the Bible in a courtroom and promise to tell the truth. The Bible also mentions the right hand, especially the right hand of God.

One verse in the Bible about the right hand that is very special to me is Isaiah 41:13, which says, "For I the LORD thy God will hold thy right hand, saying unto thee, Fear not; I will help thee." This verse became very special to me at a time when I was not living for the Lord as I should, at a time when I was going through a valley in my life. I felt so alone and so unable to live like I wanted to live. I felt that the Lord could never use me because of what I had done and what I was. Then I read this Scripture, and I knew that God was with me and that He wanted to help.

35

I would often close my eyes and see Him reaching down. I would feel my right hand literally lifting as if to grasp His hand. I realize now that I did not deserve God's help, nor do any of us really deserve His help. The Bible says in Isaiah 53:6a, "All we like sheep have gone astray; we have turned every one to his own way...." It is because of His faithfulness that He helps us.

GOD IS FAITHFUL TO EVERY PROMISE HE HAS EVER MADE.

II Timothy 2:13 assures, "If we believe not, yet he abideth faithful: he cannot deny himself." He is faithful because it is who He is (Deuteronomy 7:9). God is faithful to every promise He has ever made. Even when Israel was not walking with God, He was still with them. He was waiting for them to turn to Him (Isaiah 30:12). He is always waiting for us to turn to Him.

The right hand has become a reminder to me of God's faithfulness. When I hear any mention of the right hand, my mind goes to those dark days in my life, and I realize that it was His right hand reaching down to mine, waiting to take the problems that I was trying to conquer myself – in my own strength, with my own right hand – and place them into His right hand where the power is, where the compassion is, and where the strength is. Many times since, I often feel God's right hand holding me, helping me, and protecting me. I am thankful for the reminder of the "Right Hand" in my life.

I encourage you to look up other Scriptures about the right hand.

faithfulness

Today's
Date: _____

Passage

Prayers Requests

Notes

Faithful in the Everyday

By Hannah Suttle

Moreover it is required in stewards, that a man be found faithful.

I Corinthians 4:2

You have probably noticed that one person who is at church every time the doors are open. They are faithful to every church service, special meeting, soul-winning, and every ministry opportunity that arises. I personally know a lot of people like this. They come to church every day of the week to serve in various capacities with no promise of any form of tangible return, but rather, just to minister.

I remember going to another local church. When I introduced our group, a member said, "Oh! That is the church full of radical Christians. They are really overly dedicated there." Some might have taken offense to that statement, but I was so encouraged. When people look at you as a Christian, do they think, "Wow! They are really radical in their Christianity" or do they think, "They are pretty average in their walk with God"?

More importantly, I wonder what God thinks when He looks at me? Am I someone who is seeking to be faithful to honor Him in every aspect of my life, or am I simply average? Personally, I want to be far from average in my walk with Him! I definitely have not "arrived" in the area of faithfulness, but I will quickly share a few things that have been encouraging to me.

Along with the theme verse for this devotional, I would like to share Romans 12:1, which says, "I beseech you therefore, brethren, by the mercies of God, that ye present your bodies a living sacrifice, holy, acceptable unto God, which is your reasonable service." It is so easy for us to look at missionaries and put them on a pedestal because they have given up everything in their personal comfort zone to spread the Gospel. However, according to these verses, dedicating every part of your life to God is not a great sacrifice. It is reasonable; and to be found faithful, it is required.

I am not saying everyone has to be a missionary in order to be found faithful in God's eyes, but everyone must surrender their life, heart, thoughts, emotions, and will to whatever it is that God may ask them to do. My pastor once challenged me in a message with this statement, "What am I holding back from God that is hindering Him from using me?" The truth is, God does not just choose to use some people more than others. Rather, He uses those who are willing to give Him every part of their life.

Maybe you surrendered your life to the Lord at a camp service fifteen years ago, but have you surrendered today? The secret to being faithful to God fifty years from now is being faithful today. The secret to joyful Christian living is being faithful to dwell with your Savior every moment! Psalm 91:1, says, "He that dwelleth in the secret place of the most High shall abide under the shadow of the Almighty."

faithfulness

Today's
Date: _____

Passage ―――――――

Prayers Requests ―――――――

Notes ―――――――

Faithfulness in Fear

By Kelly Byrley

And when she could not longer hide him, she took him for an ark of bulrushes,
and daubed it with slime and with pitch, and put the child therein;
and she laid it in the flags by the river's brink.

Exodus 2:3

Every time I read the story of Moses, I am amazed at the faithfulness of his mother, Jochebed. What could she do to preserve the life of her child after Pharaoh ordered all male babies to be killed? She knew Moses was special, so she did what she humanly could to protect him by hiding him away. Imagine how difficult it must have been to hide an infant! I am sure she was fearful! She was putting her entire family's lives at risk, but I believe she knew the Lord had a plan for Moses, so she faithfully committed to protect him.

When she could no longer keep him hidden, she made an ark, put little baby Moses inside, and placed it in the Nile River. Can you even imagine how hard that must have been for her? He could have been eaten by a crocodile, fallen out of the ark and drowned, or been washed away never to be seen again. As a mom, I am certain Jochebed heavily considered all those scenarios, but she stuck to the plan the Lord had given her. We know the outcome, but she did not.

Remaining faithful during fearful times requires trust. It is so amazing how the Lord not only protected Moses but allowed his mom to be paid to raise him for a time! What a sweet reward! I am sure she was grateful that she stayed faithful. Although she was probably never able to fully see the end result of her faithfulness and all that the Lord did through Moses, generation after generation has been able to read about it.

So, what do we have that we need to put in the ark? What precious thing is the devil trying to rip out of our hands? When we have done all that we can, are we willing to pack it up, secure it to the best of our human abilities, and fully turn it over to the Lord to protect and sustain? Will we remain faithful to do our part to carry out God's plan for our sacred thing? We need to be faithful to consistently put our sacred things in the ark. We do not know how God will use them, but we can trust that He has a plan. An entire nation's deliverance depended on Jochebed's faithfulness, and she had no idea. She just chose to cast out fear, remain faithful, and fully follow the Lord as He directed her steps.

JOCHEBED STUCK TO THE PLAN THE LORD HAD GIVEN HER. WE KNOW THE OUTCOME, BUT SHE DID NOT.

faithfulness

Today's
Date: _____

Passage

Prayers Requests

Notes

God is Faithful

Anonymous

If we believe not, yet he abideth faithful...

2 Timothy 2:13a

God's faithfulness is sure. It is not dependent upon our belief or acceptance. This truth remains. God is faithful! He will keep His promises. Every. Single. Time.

During one of the many voyages the disciples took with Jesus, He said to them, "Let us go to the other side" (Luke 8:23b). As they sailed, Jesus fell asleep, and a storm of wind overtook the ship. The disciples were in jeopardy, the situation was desperate, and they feared for their lives as the ship filled with water. While the circumstances continued to overcome them, they cried out in fear declaring that they were going to perish. Amid the turmoil, their minds had forgotten the Lord's promise of going "to the other side." Despite their lack of faith, Jesus calmed the storm and brought peace to their situation. They arrived at their destination just as Jesus had said. Although they doubted and believed not, the Lord remained faithful and kept His word.

How many times do our circumstances cause us to question whether our survival is possible? We grasp for faith while looking for a glimmer of hope and allow our vision to be clouded by the fierceness of the storm. Our minds wander from the truth of the Scriptures. We doubt His presence and question His promises, yet He abides faithful. He cannot deny Himself. He is right there as "a very present help in trouble" (Psalm 46:1). He will not leave us or forsake us.

God is faithful, dear friend! His Word will not fail. Even if defeat seems apparent, if it seems like life's storms will drown you, or the mountain you are facing seems impossible to climb, God is faithful! He will not, He cannot, fail! His promises are always true. Though Abraham waited long for a son and Joseph sat forgotten in Pharaoh's prison, our God proved Himself faithful in keeping His Word. He is the same yesterday, today, and forever. He was faithful to the saints of old, and He will be to us. Every. Single. Time.

faithfulness

Passage

Today's
Date: _____

Prayers Requests

Notes

The Greatest Faithfulness

By Julie Payne

... I will never leave thee, nor forsake thee.

Hebrews 13:5b

The Lord's Faithfulness is very special to me. Hebrews 13:5b says, "... I will never leave thee, nor forsake thee." This verse was used to comfort me as a young girl when I was away with a friend and her family on a camping trip. While on that trip, I struggled with the syndrome of "homesickness." I am so thankful that those I was with had the wisdom to help me with God's Word, and to remind me of His faithfulness.

Through the years of my life, I have also had other moments of greatly appreciating God's faithfulness. To know that the God of Heaven is always there for us is just a blessing that is hard to compare to anything else! There are many areas wherein God proves His faithfulness in our lives; let us look at a few:

In Life

We are alive! We have survived another day and have "lived to tell about it." Acts 17:28a states, "For in him we live, and move, and have our being ...." His faithfulness is why

we

HIS
FAITHFULNESS
HAS
CONTINUED
FROM THE
BEGINNING
UNTIL NOW.

are here! He not only gave us life, but He is the One Who keeps it in us. Psalm 119:90 says, "Thy faithfulness is unto all generations: thou hast established the earth, and it abideth." His faithfulness has continued from the beginning until now and will continue for those in the future. Oh, what a promise!

In Temptations

I Corinthians 10:13b states, "...but God is faithful, who will not suffer you to be tempted above that ye are able ...." When temptations come, be assured the faithful God will always be there to keep you from falling into any tempting area you face! II Thessalonians 3:3 tells us, "But the Lord is faithful, who shall stablish you, and keep you from evil." Again, His faithfulness is there to keep us strong!

In Discouragement

Lamentations 3:22-23 tells us that even in very hard times, the Lord is faithful. "It is of the LORD'S mercies that we are not consumed because his compassions fail not. They are new every morning: great is thy faithfulness." God's faithfulness is described through the Psalms as well. In Psalm 46:1, "God is our refuge and strength, a very present help in trouble." Being there as a very present help is great proof of His faithfulness! Then in Psalm 89:1, "I will sing of the mercies of the LORD for ever: with my mouth will I make known thy faithfulness to all generations." His Faithfulness is stated again throughout the chapter, and in verse 33 it says, "Nevertheless my lovingkindness will I not utterly take from him, nor suffer my faithfulness to fail." Despite the trouble, heartache, and discouragement, the Lord proves faithful! Remember, God is not a respecter of persons; He will be there for us as well.

Oh, how I love and am amazed at God's faithfulness! He proved Himself faithful to me as the little homesick girl, and He has proven it to me time and time again in my life. Thank You, Lord, for Your great faithfulness!

faithfulness

Today's
Date: _____

Passage

Prayers Requests

Notes

How To Be Faithful For Fifty Years

By Susan Hutchens

But the Lord is faithful, who shall stablish you, and keep you from evil.

2 Thessalonians 3:3

As I write this, my dad has just celebrated fifty years of being saved. He was twenty-seven when he was saved, and he had not been in church nor known any saved people up to that point. He recalls when a friend of his was celebrating being saved for ten years. Daddy was amazed that someone could stay in church for ten years! He could not imagine that he would be in church that long!

Now, it has been fifty years. He has been in church and faithfully serving the Lord for all that time. When he was saved on January 26, 1972, my dad did not look down the road and vow to serve God for the next fifty years. He just knew that God had saved him, and he set out to serve Him that day.

How does a Christian aspire to be faithful for fifty years? The short answer: you do not!

The first thing to remember is that God is the One who is faithful. 2 Thessalonians 3:3 says, "But the Lord is faithful, who shall stablish you, and keep you from evil." It is only by His faithfulness that any of us begin or continue serving Him. He has promised us eternal life and to be present with us every day, and that He will preserve us and strengthen us. And He is faithful! He will keep His promises! But we do not magically stay faithful without having some purpose to be faithful! Joshua 24:15 instructs us to "choose you this day whom ye will serve," so we have a choice in being faithful. That choice is a daily choice.

Today, choose to ... Read your Bible. Pray over your day. Obey God in the moment of temptation. Be like Jesus in how you treat others. Trust God when bad news comes. Go to church when the doors are open. Be different from the world. Allow your mind to be renewed by God. Die to self.

Today, be faithful today. Then, be faithful tomorrow. As you are faithful each day, you will have an unbroken string of days that will become weeks and months, and years. And one day, you will look back over a life well-lived in faithfulness to God for five years, ten years, twenty years, or maybe even fifty years! And you will tell others how faithful God has been, and how they can faithfully serve Him too!

Name some ways you can be faithful today. How will you take specific actions to choose faithfulness today?

faithfulness

Passage

Today's
Date: _____

Prayers Requests

Notes

Never Ending Faithful-ness

By Renee Patton

Thy mercy, O Lord, is in the heavens;
and thy faithfulness reacheth unto the clouds.

Psalm 36:5

Can we touch the clouds? Of course not! Thus, we could never reach the end of God's faithfulness to us! I love to look at the clouds! I love cloudy days! They remind me of God's imminent return. While I reach out to the clouds and cannot touch them, I know they are there just as I know God is there even though I cannot see Him.

Since the time of my salvation, I have seen God show Himself faithful to me and countless others through answered prayer, unexpected blessings, and so much more. So why then would I not remain faithful? Perhaps hurt, anger or bitterness creeps in and begins to distance us from God. The one thing to remember is that God never moves. It is always us who moves from Him. At times, we all have things, if we are not careful, that will pause our faithfulness to God.

61

However, this brings the promise of II Chronicles 30:9b to mind, "... for the Lord your God is gracious and merciful, and will not turn away his face from you if ye return to him." No matter what I do, You, Lord, will always be there! Unlike man, You are eternal, unending, never ceasing, and forever faithful!

GOD IS ALWAYS FAITHFUL.

I will be honest, there are countless times I have pondered God's faithfulness to Israel. Yet, this is a prime example of us with God. No matter the degree of my sin, God is always faithful. There may be earthly consequences, but God is faithful through every step. God continually forgives and embraces His chosen ones – just as He continually forgives and embraces us!

Just as the clouds are unreachable, so is God's faithfulness to us! How has God been faithful to me?

faithfulness

Today's
Date: _____

Passage ―――――

Prayers Requests ―――――

Notes ―――――

Faithfulness in Praise

By Wanda Davidson

Great is the Lord, and greatly to be praised; and his greatness is unsearchable.

Psalms 145:3

The song, "I Am No Stranger to Grace," says, "My first thought this morning was of my great riches, what substance, such treasures, the morning did bring. There was joy beyond telling, a hope beyond failing, I'm acquainted with all these things." Contemplating those words starts a great stirring in my soul. No, I am not rich in money or worldly goods; what I have is far greater! My Heavenly Father has given me a Book of promises, the Bible, that is all mine! Bless the Lord, oh my soul, bless His holy name!

The key to being faithful in praise is in the first words of that song – "my first thought this morning." Our first thoughts ought to be toward God and His faithfulness. Every man since the beginning of time has experienced the faithfulness of God by watching the sunrise. He gives every breath and a measure of health to go about the workday. Recognizing God's goodness and faithfulness in our lives should create a thankful heart in us. In Psalm 145:2, King David, the great songwriter of praise, said, "Every day will I bless thee...."

65

The Gospels of Matthew and Luke tell us to consider the lilies of the field and how much more God desires to bless us. Considering brings praise to God rather than complaints to Him. God promised Israel a land flowing with milk and honey for which they did not buy nor work. He brought them on their journey with daily miracles. But because they failed to consider and praise, they turned into complainers and only two of that great number received the promise. Joshua tells us that not one thing failed of all the good things that God had promised them. God had remained faithful to His Word even though only two of them claimed it!

When we consider the faithfulness of God and His greatness in our lives and become faithful in praise to Him, our own conversation and countenance will change. God inhabits praise! What a wonderful spiritual cycle to develop! Praise God, He shows up, and I become more like Him because I have been in His presence!

faithfulness

Today's
Date: _____

Passage

Prayers Requests

Notes

hf

It Is All in His Hands

By Catherine Aylor

They are new every morning: great is thy faithfulness.

Lamentations 3:23

God, I don't know why this is happening in my life,

The unforeseen circumstances and all the strife.

I thought through faithfulness I would be carried through,

Not to be looked upon as an outcast and visions construed.

You see I make mistakes each day.

I mess up so much along the way.

I face battles and don't always make the right choice.

When I am not around, some may not hear my voice.

The one that is there and praising through the storm.

The one that is there and realizes what You saved me from.

The one that realizes I am nothing without You.

The one that knows You will bring me through this too.

The one that screams, "I don't know how to do this."

The one that shouts out, "Okay, Lord, that mark I missed."

The one that cries in the quiet and in the night.

The one that smiles in front of others, so they know I am alright.

NOTHING WE FACE CAN OUTWEIGH HIS FAITHFULNESS.

The one that doesn't know which way to turn.

When faced with battles, I have continued and learned.

Lord, it amazes me that you are still here to listen to me.

When others don't realize the hurt that they don't see.

Lord, it is only You – the reason I can make it through.

The reason I don't give up is solely because of You!

I have faced many difficult roads and made it because of Your help, I know.

I have looked at others and wished for their easy road on which to go!

Then, I realize if You didn't think I could handle this trial,

You would have taken it from me after a short while.

Yet it is lingering, and the pain is so great to endure,

The weight of it all, how could I possibly handle more?

Then, the still small voice on which I Stand!

REMINDS ME... IT'S ALL IN HIS HANDS!

Thank you, Lord, for allowing me to live this life,

Along with the trials and all the strife.

I couldn't imagine having it so easy and not being able to realize it is You.

Every circumstance I face, I made it in Your hands right through.

Great is Your faithfulness through every trial.

Great is Your faithfulness up every mountain and along every mile.

Great is Your faithfulness and in Whom I put my trust for sure.

Great is Your faithfulness.

In Your hands will I continue to endure!

I challenge you to read Lamentations 3 today. It is a great chapter, but if you will not read it, at least read the following excerpt taken from

Chapter 3. Lamentations 3:20-23 says, "My soul hath them still in remembrance, and is humbled in me. This I recall to my mind, therefore have I hope. It is of the Lord's mercies that we are not consumed because his compassions fail not. They are new every morning: great is thy faithfulness."

God will never leave nor forsake. Nothing we face can outweigh His faithfulness. Look up the song "Great is Thy Faithfulness" and read the words carefully. If you can listen, spend a few minutes and ponder the words. If you are going through a trial right now, realize that there have been many days that you have had joy. Think on those times and ask the Lord to renew your joy through His faithfulness. Allow Him to help give you peace and strength for this trial. If you are not going through a trial or a storm, thank the Lord for His faithfulness. Ask Him to bring it to mind in the next valley you face. We can live this life in the "craziness of times" because "It is all in His hands" and because... Great is Thy faithfulness.

faithfulness

Today's
Date: _____

Passage

Prayers Requests

Notes

He Abideth Faithful

By Elizabeth Garrett

If we believe not, yet he abideth faithful: he cannot deny himself.

II Timothy 2:13

We often speak of God's faithfulness to us, but have we ever stopped to actually define the word "faithful"? According to Strong's concordance, the word "faithful" as used here in II Timothy 2:13 means, "Trustworthy, sure, true."

As I considered this verse, the person who came to mind was Sarah, the wife of Abraham. God appeared unto Abraham in Ur of the Chaldees and commanded him to leave his country and his kindred to go to a land that God would show him. God made a covenant with Abraham, promising that He would make Abraham a great nation and that in him all the families of the earth would be blessed.

Now, all the promises that God made Abraham depended on a son. However, we are told in Scripture that Sarah was barren. The years continued to pass, and Sarah remained barren. Finally, she told Abraham to go to her Egyptian servant, Hagar. Abraham heeded his wife's counsel, and Ishmael was born. Yet this was not God's plan! Sarah had lost faith that God would keep His Word and tried to find a solution to what she considered a problem.

God appeared to Abraham again and reminded him of the promise, "I will certainly return unto thee according to the time of life; and, lo, Sarah thy wife shall have a son" (Genesis 18:10). At the time appointed, the Lord visited Sarah, and she conceived and bore a son. This son was Isaac, the son of promise, born to Abraham at one hundred years old!

Hebrews 11:11 says, "Through faith also Sara herself received strength to conceive seed, and was delivered of a child when she was past age, because she judged him faithful who had promised." The last phrase caught my attention. She judged God to be faithful, trustworthy, sure, and true. There were times when Sarah struggled to believe; when she felt that God would not fulfill His promise. She even attempted to "fix" the situation herself. But, in the end, she judged God to be faithful, and God proved His faithfulness by keeping His promise.

God abideth faithful, even during those times when we struggle to believe. He is always trustworthy, even when we are not trustworthy. Isaiah tells us that God's thoughts and ways are far above our own. The Lord does not work according to my plans or my timetable. However, I can trust in the fact that He is faithful. What He has promised, He will do in spite of those moments of weakness when I lose faith.

Are you facing a difficulty and wondering if God will keep His Word? Can we trust Him even when we cannot see the way or understand what is happening in our lives? Yes! Even if we do not believe, God abideth faithful, He cannot deny Himself. He cannot turn back on His Word. May He grant us the faith to trust in Him!

faithfulness

Today's
Date: _____

Passage ―――――

Prayers Requests ―――――

Notes ―――――

Faithful Despite Feelings

By Hannah Kasprzyk

Saying, Father, if thou be willing, remove this cup from me:
nevertheless not my will, but thine, be done.

Luke 22:42

May I be honest? I do not always feel like doing the things I know I should. Have you ever felt this way before? Growing up, there were times I did not want to go to my church's weekly Friday night teen activities. Nevertheless, I always attended. My mother would encourage me by saying "bring the fun with you" as I walked out the door. Without realizing it, I was learning the concept of being faithful. Faithfulness is being dependable regardless of how you feel. Too often, we let our emotions dictate our actions instead of the other way around.

When Jesus was in the Garden of Gethsemane, He prayed three times asking God the Father to let the cup of suffering and pain of the crucifixion pass from Him. At that moment in His flesh, Jesus did not feel like dying on the cross. Luke 22:44 says, "And being in an agony he prayed more earnestly: and his sweat was as it were great drops of blood falling down to the ground." Regardless of how He felt, Jesus still submitted Himself to the will of His Father when He said "nevertheless, not my will, but thine be done" (Luke 22:42b). Jesus remained faithful even unto the death of the cross.

If you have not experienced it already, there will come times in life when you do not feel like doing what you know is expected or required of you. You may get tired or be burdened down with so many responsibilities that you do not think you can go on. At times like these, pray and submit your will to God's will. Paul said in Philippians 4:13, "I can do all things through Christ which strengtheneth me." Despite how you feel, you can be faithful to Christ by submitting to His will and seeking His strength.

When God looks at your life, does He see someone who is faithful? It is not always easy, and it is not always what you feel like doing, but the Lord promises in Proverbs 28:20a, "A faithful man shall abound with blessings...."

faithfulness

Today's
Date: _____

Passage

Prayers Requests

Notes

Finding Us Faithful

By Sharon Garrett

Moreover it is required in stewards, that a man be found faithful.

I Corinthians 4:2

I had carefully planned Vacation Bible School and had the workers in place. Since it was a new church, and we had only a few experienced workers, I was counting on them. The Sunday before VBS started, one of the workers notified me that she would not be there the first three days of that week. She told me that her family invited her out of town to celebrate her recent graduation. I was stunned – she was the one worker with the most experience, so I was relying on her. When I could finally speak, I asked her if maybe she could not wait another week since she had promised her help and the plans for VBS had been made months before. She replied that she had notified her family that she would be there that afternoon. She was leaving me in a very difficult position. Faithful? Definitely not! But how many times do we fail to be faithful to what God has asked us to do? Many times, we respond with "Oh, He will understand."

God, in His Word, has much to say about faithfulness. The verse above, I Corinthians 4:2 says, "Moreover it is required (necessary to be done) in stewards, (one who manages affairs for another; in this case, our Savior), to be faithful." As stewards, God has committed to our trust certain responsibilities. It can be talents (Matthew 25:19-28), spiritual gifts (I Corinthians 12:4-11), or commands that God has given us.

God says in Psalms 101:6, "Mine eyes shall be upon the faithful of the land, that they may dwell with me." "Most men will proclaim every one his own goodness: but a faithful man who can find?" (Proverbs 20:6). Luke 16:10a, "He that is faithful in that which is least is faithful also in much ...." Most people are ready to serve in a place of eminence but do not wish to serve in a lowly position. We should be faithful in every job that is given to us.

There are people in the Bible mentioned as faithful. The meaning of "faithful" is to be firm in adherence to promises; observance of duty. In Colossians 1:7, Epaphras is mentioned as "our dear fellowservant, who is for you a faithful minister." Tychius was "a beloved brother, and a faithful minister" (Colossians 4:7; Ephesians 6:21). In Galatians 3:9, Abraham is called faithful. Hebrews 3:2b says, "... Moses was faithful in all his house." I Peter 5:12a says, "By Silvanus, a faithful brother unto you...."

We all desire to hear our Savior say, "Well done, thou good and faithful servant." But are we faithful? Can God depend on us to fulfill our duties? Can our Pastor and church leaders depend on us when we are in charge of some part of the ministry? Do we make excuses when we are asked to do something at church? Just how faithful are we?

faithfulness

Today's
Date: _____

Passage _____

Prayers Requests _____

Notes _____

Great is Thy Faithfulness

By Kay Reese

*It is of the Lord's mercies that we are not consumed, because his compassions
fail not. They are new every morning: great is thy faithfulness.*

Lamentations 2:22-23

A teacher and poet, Thomas Chisholm wrote down the words to this
popular hymn. It was set to music some time afterward, and today, it
is a very beloved song. The words are a testimony to the unchanging
faithfulness of God.

The word "faithfulness" means to show off a fact or a quality of being
true to one's word of commitment. In all that our awesome Creator has
placed upon this earth, we see a reflection of His faithful character.
The sun rises and sets with each new day, and we think nothing of it
happening over again. The oceans push and pull; the rivers flow and
go at His command. These join all nature in manifold witness of His
faithfulness.

All we have needed, His hand hath provided! The greatest act of all
is the promise of His only Son to die for all mankind and to raise Him
to life again.

Christian ladies, His wonderful example draws us to be faithful. He lives in our hearts and His attributes will be revealed in our lives. We learn to love, respect, give, be patient and understanding, and to serve Him. Through His faithfulness, we can learn to take life, the good and the bad. We are sure that what He has promised He will do! We long in our lives to be faithful as He is.

Oh Lord, help us as servants to show forth Thy faithfulness in our lives! Thank you, for all the promises and witnesses You have given to guide us.

IN ALL THAT OUR AWESOME CREATOR HAS PLACED UPON THIS EARTH, WE SEE A REFLECTION OF HIS FAITHFUL CHARACTER.

faithfulness

Today's
Date: _____

Passage _____

Prayers Requests _____

Notes _____

Will You Be Missed

By Julianna Poindexter

Therefore my beloved brethren, be ye steadfast, unmovable, always abounding in the work of the Lord, forasmuch as ye know that your labour is not in vain in the Lord.

1 Corinthians 15:58

Will you be missed? I have heard many pastors ask the question along the lines of, "whenever you are gone, will you be missed?" This statement is typically made when they are preaching on the topic of service in the church. Let us ask ourselves that question today.

Whenever you are gone from the church you are now in (whether it be through death or moving to a new location), will you be missed? Will people even notice that you are not there? Will there be holes to fill?

As Christians, we are not called to be pew ornaments. We are called to be faithful servants. Are you a dependable, faithful servant at the place you worship every week? Are you striving to make your church a better place? Are you looking to be served? Or are you looking to serve and help others?

I encourage you to go read I Corinthians 12. This chapter explains how important it is for every single church member to be involved in making the church body better! We know that the Lord has given every one of us specific things that we can do and in which we thrive to better our churches for His glory. For some, it may be singing or teaching. But for others, it may be things like serving or just being an encouragement. It is your job to find out where you fit best and plug into it immediately!

Let us strive to be those church members that make a difference! As a pastor's daughter, I am glad to say that I can recall many faithful people we have labored with throughout the years! Some are still with us, some are with the Lord now, and others have gone on to minister in different parts of the world. Not only were they such an encouragement to us as a pastor's family, but they were faithful and dedicated in everything that they did around the house of God. Our church would not be what it is today without those individuals and families!

If you cannot think of any areas that you are faithfully involved in at your local church, change that today! Go talk to your pastor or pastor's wife about it. You would be surprised at the number of things there are to do around the church. Find somewhere to plug in, and then stick with it! Be the most faithful servant that you can be for the glory of God. It will not go unnoticed!

faithfulness

Passage

Today's
Date: _____

Prayers Requests

Notes

The Resources of the Righteous

By Candance Voyles

And he shall be like a tree planted by the rivers of water, that bringeth forth his fruit in his season; his leaf also shall not wither; and whatsoever he doeth shall prosper.

Psalms 1:3

Have you ever had an MRI? Do you enjoy that experience? Let me tell you, I do not! I am not sure why. Perhaps it is a response to a trauma in my life in recent years, but I have developed some claustrophobia. That makes the experience very unpleasant, to say the least! To get through it, I began to quote Bible verses in my head and really meditate and visualize them. My mind settled on Psalm 1.

I began to imagine that tree that the psalmist is comparing to the righteous, as it is planted by the rivers of water. I imagined those roots spreading under the ground finding nutrients. Its leaves spread out in the spring. I imagined that fruit coming forth and those leaves changing in the fall and those branches shaking in the winter cold. Before I knew it, the test was over, and the truth of God's Word had sustained me

WE HAVE A SOURCE OF POWER.

through another uncomfortable, although short, ordeal as it had seen me through many longer, more painful ones.

God allowed me to see some truths from my meditation on this familiar, precious passage about the righteous and the capability that His people have, even the power we have, to remain faithful and stable through all the seasons of life.

The righteous are rooted (Colossians 2:6-7). We have a Source of power the ungodly do not have. We do not have to live a roller coaster Christian life in the energy of the flesh. That energy will all too quickly give out on us. What is our relationship with His Word? Are we tapping into that strength regularly, not out of obligation or routine, but out of genuine hunger and thirst for righteousness? God's Word will sustain us! It will not do that for the ungodly. Psalm 1:4b says they are "... like the chaff which the wind driveth away" – no roots. Nothing to hold them during the storm. The truth of God's Word will stand. That Truth may not always change our feelings. But, praise God, feelings will not change the Truth either! It will hold us no matter what comes!

The righteous have rivers. We have the Comforter of God (the Holy Spirit), the children of God (the saints), and the call to God (our prayer life) to tap into. These give refreshment to our needy soul to remain faithful during the dark days, the dry days. The righteous have a redeemer. Psalm 1:6a says, "the LORD knoweth...." He knows. He sees. He cares. If we keep our eyes on our Redeemer and not on the storm, He can help us to remain consistent.

The righteous have a rescue and a reward. The end of Psalm 1:3 states, "... bringeth forth his fruit in his season; his leaf also shall not wither; and whatsoever he doeth shall prosper." That does not mean everything is going to be perfect, but we can bring forth fruit and have a purpose. Our lives will not be barren, and we can serve with stability. There is an eternal reward. The reward of hearing, "Well done, thou good and faithful servant."

The only way we can remain faithful to Him is to tap into the resources, those vast riches of grace, and find sustenance. That tree went through seasons. Beautiful spring – new life! It experienced fall – a time of reaping and rejoicing. It also experienced harsh winters and maybe dry summers. It had to depend on what it was given in the mild seasons to sustain it during the harsher seasons. The seasons changed, but the tree remained rooted and near the rivers. I encourage you today, tap into your Resource, the One who has been made righteous. That is the only way we can serve with stability and finish well.

faithfulness

Today's
Date: _____

Passage _____

Prayers Requests _____

Notes _____

Well Done, Thou Good and Faithful Servant!

By Deborah South

Well done, thou good and faithful servant:
thou hast been faithful over a few things ....

Matthew 25:21b

What Christian does not want to hear these words from the Lord: "Well done, thou good and faithful servant?"

As I have gotten older, I have seen many great men and ladies of God pass away. The past two years have been the hardest for me as I saw people pass away that I had watched over the years. I had seen their lives. I had personal relationships with them. I had entertained them in my home. Now they are gone. I have no doubt that when they arrived in Heaven, they heard the Lord say, "Well done, thou good and faithful servant." They left behind a legacy of being both good and faithful! They were great examples of godliness.

We see faithfulness in action around us every day in those Christians (husband, pastor, Sunday School teacher, Christian school teacher, godly church member, etc.) who stand for the truth of the Word of

101

God. I was blessed with an example of faithfulness in my parents. I have watched them stand for the Lord for many years.

When my dad was first saved, I was five years old. I watched the change in his life. I watched God change a hard man into a faithful man of God. My dad had many challenges in his life that could have made him quit on God, but he remained faithful. He went to Bible college as a young adult with a wife and three children during the recession of 1975. He could not find a job. My mom was expecting baby number five. It was not easy during those times. But my dad told my mom, "God brought me to Bible college, and I am not going to quit until He leads me differently." My mom stood with him faithfully, and they just kept living for God. After Bible college, my dad pastored in Georgia for thirty-three years. He and Mom were not perfect, but they were faithful.

In these later years of my parents' lives (Dad is eighty, Mom is seventy-seven), they still have not quit. They represent a printing ministry out of the same church my dad pastored, which is now pastored by my brother. They are leaving behind a legacy of faithfulness for me to follow. I cannot imagine if my parents decided today that serving God all those years was not worth it; that it was time to change what they taught me over the years. I would be devastated and, no doubt, others that their lives have touched would be hurt as well.

Is there someone you could encourage and thank for their faithful example? Are you being faithful to the Lord? Is someone watching and learning from your testimony? One day, will we hear the words, "Well done, thou good and faithful servant?"

faithfulness

Today's
Date: _____

Passage

Prayers Requests

Notes

Faithful To The End

By Beverley Wells

And if it seem evil unto you to serve the LORD, choose you this day whom ye will serve; whether the gods which your fathers served that were on the other side of the flood, or the gods of the Amorites, in whose land ye dwell: but as for me and my house, we will serve the LORD.

Joshua 24:15

Where do I start? The only place I can think to start is when God the Father sent his only begotten Son into this world to save lost sinners in need of salvation (John 3:16). This is our example of faithfulness! Jesus, the son of God, left His heavenly home to come to a sin-cursed world in the form of a baby in a virgin's womb to die for mankind, that we might live. Jesus was faithful to fulfill the Father's wishes.

It was His privilege to honor the Father in His sacrifice. Take a moment and read of the faithfulness of the Lord in Romans 10. It might be that within these pages you too will remember the Lord and His faithfulness to you. If at some point you find yourself in need of what the Scriptures say, you will be exactly where you need to be to find the answer of faithfulness.

I thank the Lord for the day that the preaching of the Word opened my eyes to my need of salvation. My faith became real! Not only did it become real, but it also became personal. Amen! No more restless nights fearing hell and its eternal damnation. No more fearing beyond the grave and eternal darkness. My viewpoint on life had changed. It was different, like day to night. I desired to please the Lord. That was the least that I could do for the price that He paid for this wretched sinner. Oh, what a change! New life in Him brought such peace!

As a new babe in Christ, the Lord quickly showed me how faithful He was to me outside of salvation, as if that was not enough: supplying the financial needs when funds were short, sending clothing and food when needed, thousands of dollars supplied for medical bills when I had cancer, etc. ... the list goes on. To some, it may sound silly or like a coincidence, but I know from Whom all these came. It was from my faithful Lord. He knew my need when I did not ask Him for it. He supplied just in time, proving to me His faithfulness.

These experiences seem like just yesterday. You may be in those phases of life, or you may be like I am now, needing faithfulness in other areas. Because of the past, I know He will be faithful to me now and in my future. Colossians 3:23 became so real as our children got older. This verse became a faithful reminder to keep things in perspective. It states..."And whatsoever ye do, do it heartily, as to the Lord, and not unto men ...."

It became necessary to recite to them, "as unto the Lord," quietly reminding them and myself that how we respond and what we do is unto the Lord, not to man. When we grow tired "in well-doing," when we are treated wrongly or in other difficult situations, we must respond faithfully to the Lord. It is our reasonable service.

Sadly, I fall short just as many of you do. Start anew just like you did when Christ saved you. Kindle the fires of faithfulness. Stay in His Word. Listen to the preaching of His Word. Listen to godly music. Get godly counsel. Remain faithful to the house of God. Remain in the convictions and standards of His Word. Be a Joshua – "As for me and my house we will serve the Lord!" His word is faithful! May your prayer and song be, "Faithful to the End."

faithfulness

Today's
Date: _____

Passage
_____

Prayers Requests
_____

Notes
_____

Find Us Faithful

By Ashley Thompson

Most men will proclaim every one his own goodness:
but a faithful man who can find?

Proverbs 20:6

We all know and have sung the hymn, "Great is Thy Faithfulness" dozens of times, and we do not doubt its truth. God is faithful. Always! He has never failed us, and He never will. The question is, how is our faithfulness toward God? Every Christian wants to hear God say, "Well done, thy good and faithful servant." Will you hear God say this?

Moses, David, and Daniel are a few men that are referred to in the Bible as faithful. Were they perfect? No. Sinless? Far from it! The definition of faithful is, "steadfast in affection or allegiance: loyal." These men made mistakes, in fact, quite a few. Yet, God in His Word calls them faithful! God does not expect perfection. He is faithful to forgive; He just needs us to be vessels, willing to faithfully follow in His will.

As I have gotten older, many friends I grew up with have left church. They have given up on the Christian life, and many of them were people I never imagined would turn away from God! What happened? Their affection changed. They lost sight of God.

For some, it was not even that they got caught up in some great sin; it was just simply that they got distracted by the earthly affairs of life. The reality is it is easy to do. If we are not taking care of our daily walk with God and giving Him our affection and total allegiance, we could easily fall away. It takes work. It is something we have to prioritize daily – staying faithful to God and submitting to His will. It is not always the easy thing to do, but at the end of it all, it is what matters most. Psalms 31:23b says, "... the LORD preserveth the faithful...." Proverbs 28:20a says, "A faithful man shall abound with blessings...." I do not want to look back with regret! I want to live with God's blessings on my life!

IF WE ARE NOT TAKING CARE OF OUR DAILY WALK WITH GOD AND GIVING HIM OUR AFFECTION AND TOTAL ALLEGIANCE, WE COULD EASILY FALL AWAY.

faithfulness

Today's
Date: _____

Passage ——————

Prayers Requests ——————

Notes ——————

Finish...Don't Quit.

By Rachel Wyatt

I have fought a good fight, I have finished my course, I have kept the faith:

II Timothy 4:7

My dad, who pastored the same church for over thirty-five years, had people often ask him what the secret was for staying so long in the same place. His response was, "Learn to survive the quitting places."

My husband and I were recently discussing a certain missionary family in our city who had left Tanzania and returned to their home country. This family had felt that the Lord was moving them on in life, so when they returned to Tanzania from a home assignment, they decided that this would be their last year on the field. We were discussing what a beautiful transition they had experienced in their new stage of life. They had a whole year to finish their work. They were able to properly transition their work over to others, say goodbye to friends that they had made through the years of living here and take the time to find good closure on this stage of their life. Although this family was leaving the mission field to return home, they had finished ... not quit.

FINISHING
IS DONE
OUT OF
DETERMINATION,
CONFIDENCE.
AND FAITH.

We often start something, and then halfway through, we decide that it is not something that we want to be doing. Many times, we have just begun to hit the hard work part and decide that we want to give up. Things are not working out like we thought they would, and we are tempted to quit. I would encourage you to keep going and "survive the quitting places."

However, I am not saying that once you start something you should continue that thing for the rest of your life. There is nothing wrong with stopping something. What I am encouraging you to do is to finish, not quit. Set a finish line for yourself and do not quit until you have reached that goal. Maybe it is a diet that you have started and then decide that it is not working for you. Set a date that you are going to reach before you stop your diet.

Maybe your child has started taking piano lessons, and you realize that this is not something that he or she is enjoying or will excel at. Do not just let them quit. Set a goal and let them finish. Tell them, "We are going to finish this piano book you are working through, and then we will be done." Maybe you are teaching a Sunday School class, and you feel like you need to move on. I would encourage you to talk to your pastor about it and find out how you can finish well and transition the class to someone else.

Quitting makes you feel like you failed at something. Finishing makes you feel like you accomplished something.

Quitting stops you at a low point. Finishing stops you at a high point.

Quitting makes you feel like you never want to attempt anything again. Finishing sets you up to try something new.

Quitting leaves things undone. Finishing accomplishes a task.

Quitting is done out of discouragement, frustration, or fear. vQuitting is often done without counsel or prayer. Finishing is usually done with much counsel and prayer.

Often, if we are tempted to quit but instead set a finish goal, we will pass through the discouraging time and decide to just keep going! Whatever it is in your life right now that you are considering stopping, determine that you are not going to quit, but rather finish!

faithfulness

Today's
Date: _____

Passage

Prayers Requests

Notes

Faithful, not Fainting

By Marissa Patton

Therefore seeing we have this ministry, as we have received mercy, we faint not;

II Corinthians 4:1

Others are watching you. Now, just saying that sounds a bit creepy, but let's be real. We see others. Others see us. We have a sphere of influence. I see when others are faithful to God's work. I see when others are faithful to biblical standards. I see when others choose Christ even in the hard times.

I also see when others faint. I see when they choose the pleasures of the world. I see when they compromise the values they once taught and lived by. I see when others fail to remember God's faithfulness in a time when their faithfulness to God is tested. Paul encouraged the church at Corinth not to faint in their ministry. When I see others faint in ministry, it impacts my heart. Faithfulness is not easy, but it is impactful. You can make or break someone else's relationship with God.

Now, my faithfulness to God is my responsibility, not yours. However, when I see people waver in their faith, it does hurt my heart.

It causes discouragement. It sometimes causes bitterness (Hebrews 12:15). When I see others staying faithfully, it causes my heart to be joyful knowing that I am not the only one serving God. Elijah felt all alone for a time in I Kings 19:14. God reminded him of the thousands of people still bowing only to the Lord. Those prophets' faithfulness gave Elijah strength and encouragement.

I want to challenge you to stay faithful. In times of sheer weakness, remember that others are watching you. You are an influence. You can be impactful on their walk with God for the positive or negative. Choose to remain faithful and not to faint in your convictions or in God's Word. Watch how He blesses you for it.

Take time to write down a few people that you know you impact on a daily basis with your testimony – spouse, children, co-worker, church member, student, etc. Now, take time to pray that your testimony to them will be one of faithfulness.

faithfulness

Today's
Date: _____

Passage

Prayers Requests

Notes

Being Faithful While Waiting

By Jenny Young

And she vowed a vow, and said, O LORD of hosts, if thou wilt indeed look on the affliction of thine handmaid, and remember me, and not forget thine handmaid, but wilt give unto thine handmaid a man child, then I will give him unto the LORD all the days of his life, and there shall no razor come upon his head. And they rose up in the morning early, and worshipped before the LORD, and returned, and came to their house to Ramah: and Elkanah knew Hannah his wife; and the LORD remembered her.

I Samuel 1:11,19

In society in which we live today, the word "wait" is not something most people want to hear or practice. We want everything to be instantaneous, or as quick as possible. Waiting is a virtue that is lacking in our lives. Too many times we plan our future according to what we want in our lives, and we fail to keep God in the center of our plans. When God is not kept in the center of our lives we will get discouraged, upset, and angry because we have not accomplished our goals in a predetermined time frame. Our lives would be better off if we left things in His hands and His timing because He knows what is best.

Hannah was a lady who was faithful to her husband, as well as to God. Did she have an easy life? No, for her husband's second wife, Peninnah, did everything she could to make her life miserable and hard because Hannah was barren. Thankfully, Hannah did not let what Peninnah said or did to her keep her from being faithful in what she knew to be right.

Hannah was able to stay faithful because she took her pains, her aggravation, her sorrow, her hurts, her discouragement all to the Lord, the One that knew her the best. Hannah poured everything out before the Lord, and then she left it at the altar that day in God's hands. In the next chapter of Hannah's life, we see her heart rejoicing in the Lord. Why? Because she bore a man child, and she did not let the words and actions of Peninnah determine her life. She was able to see that God was Holy, there was none else like Him, and that He is the One True Rock to build her life upon.

We say our life hasn't gone as we had planned or hoped, but that doesn't mean our life is over. Have we given our plans, our burdens, our pains to the Lord on the altar and left them there for God to help us and bless us? We must get our eyes off everyone else and get them back on God. Don't let the words and actions of others discourage us or sidetrack us from what God wants to do in our lives. Our future may not end like we planned or hoped, but if we are faithful in doing what God wants, our future will end the way God planned for it to end.

As Hannah prayed "remember me," God answered with "the Lord remembered her." God has not forgotten us. He is molding us and shaping us for what is to come in our lives. Don't give up and don't give in. Be faithful in the wait and let God do the blessing and rewarding.

Psalm 62:8 - "Trust in him at all times; ye people, pour out your heart before him: God is a refuge for us. Selah."

faithfulness

Today's
Date: _____

Passage

Prayers Requests

Notes

Stewards of Faithfulness

By Judy Rolfe

Moreover it is required in stewards, that a man be found faithful.

I Corinthians 4:2

According to this verse, faithfulness in stewards is not a choice – it is a requirement. It is the act of remaining loyal to someone or something and putting that loyalty into consistent practice no matter the extenuating circumstances. It can mean keeping one's promises and being full of faith in the sense of steady devotion to a person, thing, or concept. A faithful person is constant, dedicated, devout, staunch, and true. As stewards, we represent our Lord and Savior in this present, evil world.

Proverbs 25:19 tells us that, "confidence in an unfaithful man in time of trouble is like a broken tooth, and a foot out of joint." Ouch! A broken tooth or a foot out of joint can be very painful. An unfaithful person is disloyal, faithless, fickle, treacherous, and untrue. For example, some colonists were unfaithful to the cause of independence. Some marriage partners are unfaithful to each other. How painful!

A perfect example of disloyalty. The pain reaches deeper than words can describe.

God is ever faithful to us. I John 1:9b says, "... he is faithful and just to forgive us our sins and cleanse us from all unrighteousness" when we ask. II Timothy 2:13a says, "He abideth faithful" – even when we believe not!

> A FAITHFUL
> MAN SHALL
> ABOUND
> WITH
> BLESSINGS
> PROVERBS 28:20

Proverbs 28:20 tells us that "a faithful man shall abound with blessings...." What an awesome promise!

God has given us an amazing promise in Revelation 2:10. If we remain faithful, He has promised us a crown of life. We can only imagine what that will be like!

God has been so faithful to me. He has allowed me to serve Him since August 29, 1971. I want to remain faithful to Him so I can receive that crown of life!

faithfulness

Today's
Date: _____

Passage _____

Prayers Requests _____

Notes _____

Faithful in Serving

By Stephanie Young

And Samuel said unto Jesse, Are here all thy children? And he said, There remaineth yet the youngest, and, behold, he keepeth the sheep. And Samuel said unto Jesse, Send and fetch him: for we will not sit down till he come hither.

I Samuel 16:11

As a Christian, one of our greatest goals should be that God would say of us: "Well done thou good and faithful servant." The Bible gives us examples we can follow, and one of those is David.

When Samuel went to anoint one of Jesse's sons to be the next King of Israel, David was not there, and Samuel asked if there was another son. There was no question in Jesse's mind as to where David was – he was being faithful in keeping his father's sheep (1 Samuel 16:11).

In I Samuel 17:15b, we see David returning from Saul to his faithful duty "... to keep his father's sheep...." For some, it may not have been an important job. But it was David's job, and he was faithful to do it.

In I Samuel 17:17-20, Jesse instructs David to carry some food to his brothers and to see how they were. David, in obedience to his father, rose early in the morning to do as his father bid him. When David left, he was so faithful in keeping the sheep that he left the sheep with a keeper. He made sure the sheep were cared for even when he had other orders.

In I Samuel 17:34-35, he was faithful to protect the sheep, even if it meant he would lose his life. He fought the lion and the bear to keep the sheep safe under his care.

When David was serving King Saul by playing his harp, he took that job seriously. No matter what Saul did to him, he continued to serve Saul faithfully. In I Samuel 18:9-11, when David had to flee from Saul, David still took his position as Saul's servant seriously. He did not raise his hand against Saul, God's anointed, though Saul sought to kill him. He was a faithful servant.

When David became King, we hear of all that he did and how he followed the Lord, and that he was a man after God's own heart. But in II Samuel 11:1-5, there was a time in David's life that he was not faithful "... at the time when kings go forth to battle...." (vs. 1b). He was not where he should have been and ended up committing a sin he would be remembered for to this day. During that time, his family crumbled around him.

We all want God to say of us, "Well done, thou good and faithful servant." For those words to be said, we must be faithful in whatever job God has for us. It may seem insignificant, but someone must do it. Be faithful to sweep the corner where you are, then God can entrust you to sweep the room. Whatever God has for us to do, let us be faithful. God wants to see our faithfulness in the small things before He will give us something bigger. "Thou hast been faithful over a few things, I will make thee ruler over many things."

faithfulness

Today's
Date: _____

Passage

Prayers Requests

Notes

Lessons from the Ant

By Courtney Womack

Go to the ant, thou sluggard; consider her ways, and be wise: Which having no guide, overseer, or ruler, Provideth her meat in the summer, and gathereth her food in the harvest.

Proverbs 6:6-8

Faithful to Her Commitment

Have you ever taken the time to watch an ant work? She does not need a supervisor instructing her or constantly keeping her in line; she just does what needs to be done. She gets up, stays focused, and does her task. Each ant has a vital role in storing up for the winter, and to thrive, she needs to remain committed to her task!

God gives each and every one of us ladies different gifts and talents. Not everyone is good at teaching. Not everyone is fantastic at edifying one another through sweet notes. Some women are excellent in their care of babies, while others would much rather be with the senior saints. If God has given you a gift and you know what it is, you need to stay committed to that task! God put you doing your task just like He put Esther in Shushan. For such a time as this (Esther 4:14)!

Faithful While Carrying a Burden

Ants frequently have many obstacles. These little insects can carry 10-50 times their own body weight. They are tiny creatures and even seem feeble with their size, but God has built them to hold and accomplish big tasks. The ant refuses to allow her burden or obstacle to change her attitude or faithfulness to her task!

Our faithfulness to the Lord should never be measured on our trials or burdens. Everyone has troubles and different-sized burdens. Sometimes the weight may seem impossible, but if we have put our trust and faith in the Lord, He will help us complete our task! God knows what he has tasked you with, and He has a purpose as to why He gave you that specific burden. You just stay faithful to Him and keep your eyes on Him (Ps. 32:8), and He will make sure that your task is completed (Psalm 37:5).

Faithful to Her Colony

Ants are very dedicated to their colonies. Some ants are known for working together and having problem-solving skills with feeding the young, gathering food, and protecting the colony! When a member cannot complete a task, another ant steps right in and completes the job with efficiency and urgency.

In our lives as Christian ladies, we need to be faithful to our families, our church, and our specific ministries. God has put us where we are for a purpose. We need to make sure we are doing our best to step up and help where and when we are needed. Jesus showed us the best example of faithfulness when He died on the cross for our sins (John 3:16).

What better way to point others to Christ than being like the ant! We need to stay faithful to our commitment, burden, colony, and Christ.

faithfulness

Today's
Date: _____

Passage ————————

Prayers Requests ————————

Notes ————————

Faithfulness in Little Things

By Callie Shiflett

*And let us not be weary in well doing:
for in due season we shall reap, if we faint not.*

Galatians 6:9

Faithfulness in everyday living often involves smaller and sometimes what seems like "unimportant" tasks. These tasks require stewardship. We are to be faithful stewards of what we are given. Many times stewardship is associated with tithing, but we can be stewards of those "little tasks" that God gives us.

The verse in Luke 12 comes to mind, "For unto whomsoever much is given, of him shall be much required: and to whom men have committed much, of him they will ask the more." God loads us down daily with blessings and opportunities that we can take and use to invest into others. But these opportunities come with an amazing benefit if we use them according to God's will.

Matthew 25:21, "His Lord said unto him, Well done, thou good and faithful servant: thou hast been faithful over a few things, I will make thee ruler over many things: enter thou into the joy of thy Lord." Just as God is faithful to keep His promises (no matter how big or small) to us as His children, we should be very faithful in our commitments and promises to God, even if that commitment or ministry seems insignificant.

Although being faithful in your ministry can be exciting and fun at times, we are all human. And whether we want to admit it or not, we get tired and burnt out sometimes. We get tired of not being able to always enjoy a Sunday morning service without having to think about what we need to do at the conclusion of the service. We are not always able to properly prepare our hearts for what God has for us because we may be consumed with a ministry situation that requires our full attention. We can get tired of spending our weeknights or Saturday mornings inviting people and children to church just to hear them say, "No." Sometimes you do not even receive an answer because no one is home. This can be frustrating and discouraging for me personally.

Faithfulness is easy to explain and teach. It is much harder when you try to live it after feeling let down and tired in your ministry. We may feel as if our "well doing" just seems to go unnoticed. We may reap very little or none in comparison to the time we have invested.

When you begin to feel these stresses of ministry, think back. Look at all the times that God has allowed you to use your talents and your abilities to magnify Him. Ultimately, our faithfulness to everyday tasks is small when we look at His amazing faithfulness to us. So take a step back and think about how God can bless you in your faithfulness. Work through the tough seasons of ministry. Rejoice in the blessed seasons. Never underestimate your significance to the work of God.

faithfulness

Today's
Date: _____

Passage _____

Prayers Requests _____

Notes _____

About The Authors

Each author has been handpicked because of their testimony
of Christ. God has gifted each writer with incredibly versatile
perspectives of the Christian life. These godly ladies come from
all walks of life including pastor's wives and daughters,
missionary wives, church staff ladies, and faithful church
members. Their written words of wisdom are sure
to bless your heart.

To know more about our writers please visit:
thehighlyfavouredlife.com/our-story

Salvation Made Simple
By Renee Patton

Admit. One must first admit they are a sinner. Romans 3:10 states, "As it is written, There is none righteous, no, not one." Sin is everywhere and we all commit sin, many times without even trying. Perhaps in a conversation, we say something innocently, then realize it was not correct. That, my friend, is lying. Of course, murder is a sin that is seen and felt by those affected. However, lying is too. Jeremiah reminds one that "The heart is deceitful above all things, and desperately wicked: who can know it?" (17:9). A baby does not have to be told how to sin, it is simply in our nature. One must admit they are a sinner otherwise we make God a liar as found in I John 1:10, "If we say that we have not sinned, we make him a liar, and his word is not in us."

Believe. One must believe Jesus came to this earth to be born and die for our sins. "For God so loved the world, that he gave his only begotten Son, that whosoever believeth in him should not peish, but have everlasting life" (John 3:16). God desires that we should not perish, thus the choice is ours. God gives man the opportunity for salvation if man would take it. Romans 5:8 states "But God commendeth his love toward us, in that, while we were yet sinners, Christ died for us." Webster's 1828 Dictionary defines commendeth as entrusts or gives. So, God gave us His love through His Son, Jesus. Furthermore, Romans 5:19 shows how sin came from Adam and is made righteous through Christ, "For as by one man's disobedience [Adam] many were made sinners [mankind], so by the obedience of one [Jesus] shall many [mankind] be made righteous."

Confess. Confession is made with one's own mouth. The words must come from the person alone. Romans 10:9 talks of both confession and believing, "That if thou shalt confess with thy mouth the lord Jesus, and shalt believe in thine heart that God hath raised him from the dead, thou shalt be saved." The key is I have to confess to God. My husband or friend cannot confess for me. While God gives man the opportunity on earth, there will be a time every knee will bow and confess God is Lord, "For it is written, As I live, saith the Lord, every knee shall bow to me, and every tongue shall confess to God" (Romans 14:11).

To see more resources on salvation visit:
https://www.thehighlyfavouredlife.com/simple-salvation

If you made this decision, please contact us at *highlyfavouredlife @gmail.com.* We would love to rejoice with you in the new life you now have in Christ.